Moments of Reflection

Prayers to Accompany Essential Oils

By

Jennie Fuller

This book is dedicated to God for the gift of the plants and oils and to D. Gary Young and Mary Young for bringing these beautiful oils to us.

Table of Contents

Prayers for Single Oils

Introduction

This book synergizes the power of prayer with the power of essential oils. Essential oils range in frequency from 52 MHz to 580 MHz. Praying while applying essential oils increases the frequency of the oil by up to 15 MHz. Adding positive thoughts on average increases frequency up to 15 MHz. Combining prayer, essential oils, and positive words/thoughts can help maintain a high frequency.

I offer this book as a way to use the oils each day, while taking time to pray and connect with God as the oils are applied. The prayers are short to encourage daily use. If you only have a few seconds, to just apply the oils, I highly encourage that also, as the oils have amazing benefits on their own.

I start each prayer addressing them to God or Heavenly Father. If another word such as Divine Creator or Divine Intelligence is your preference, feel free to use the word that is most comfortable for you when addressing our Creator. As each and every person is different, please use these prayers as a starting point and adjust the wording or develop your own as you are moved.

I recommend using Young Living Essential Oils. Young Living Essential Oils have a high frequency and purity. It's important to keep your body and energy field at a high frequency. Using Young Living Essential Oils can help maintain a high frequency. They are the only essential oils I've experienced that I can feel the energy and vitality of the oils – just from holding the bottle of oil. Young Living Essential Oils contain warmth, vitality, and aliveness that you want when using essential oils. There is love in every drop. More information on the quality of Young Living Essential Oils can be found at www.seedtoseal.com

It's extremely important to use a high quality essential oil for any use – topical, diffusion, or internal. You want to breathe in or apply the therapeutic qualities of the plant oil, not chemicals or synthetic fragrances and possible carcinogens that can be in low quality oils and synthetic fragrances.

Please check the labels on the oils for the recommended use. Oils can be diffused during prayer to enhance the environment. Frankincense or Sacred Frankincense is lovely for diffusing (and applying) during prayer and meditation. Oils that are safe to apply topically can be applied with a prayer to intensify the effect.

Typical points to apply the oils on the skin are bottom of the feet, ankles, wrists, and back of neck. They can also be applied over your stomach and other areas. Be careful with the "hot" oils such as oregano. It's best to dilute "hot" oils with a carrier oil, such as V6 or coconut oil, before applying them topically, especially the first few times. Please refer to the *Gentle Babies* book or the *Essential Oils Desk Reference* book for topical application of oils for children.

If you do not have the specific oil listed with a prayer, feel free to use the oil you have available. Lavender can be used for almost all topics. It's a very intuitive and adaptable essential oil.

One way to select oils is to hold your hand over the oils and feel which oil(s) responds to you. I get God bumps (goosebumps) on my arms or the back of my neck tingles when an oil resonates with me. If you do not have the oils present, you can also read the descriptions of the oils in the YL catalog and tune in to which ones resonate with you. You can also look up typical uses of oils in the *Essential Oils Desk Reference* book.

Another aspect to consider that can assist the affect of the oils is clean eating - cutting out processed food, fast food, processed sugar, etc. Removing chemicals from your food, cleaning products, beauty products, and personal care products cleanses you and your living space. Young Living has nontoxic skin care, personal care, and cleaning products infused with essential oils. Using natural and pure products also supports a high frequency living space.

One additional benefit of keeping your frequency and your living space at a high frequency is that our DNA responds to frequency. A high frequency may support DNA.

Prayers for Specific Topics

Abundance

Dear God,

Please guide this oil through my physical body and energy field. Raise my frequency to abundant prosperity. Please help me to attract and accept an abundance of love, joy, friendship, fulfillment, and an abundant income.

In Jesus' name, I pray.

Amen.

Suggested Oils: Abundance, Ginger, Orange

Dear God,

Please guide this oil through my body to each cell. Thank You for the abundance of love, joy, friendship, and prosperity that You have blessed me with.

In Jesus' name, I pray.

Amen.

Suggested Oils: Abundance, Gratitude

Acceptance

Dear God,

Please guide this oil through my physical body and energy field. Help me to accept all aspects of my life, and be in harmony with all of Your creation.

In Jesus' name, I pray.

Amen.

Suggested Oils: Acceptance, Harmony, Rose

Alignment - Body

Dear God,

Please guide this oil through my body and energy field. Calm my mind. Bring peace to my heart. Restore alignment to all aspects of my body and being.

In Jesus' name, I pray.

Amen.

Suggested Oils: Raindrop Collection, Valor, Valor II

Alignment - Life

Dear God,

Please guide this oil through my body and energy field to help bring my body, mind, and heart into harmony and unity. Align me with the flow of life. Help me to connect with my higher purpose for this lifetime.

In Jesus' name, I pray.

Amen.

Suggested Oils: Grounding, Highest Potential, Magnify Your Purpose, Valor, Valor II

Appreciation

Dear God,

Please guide this oil through my physical body and energy field. Help me to see all of the blessings in my life. I give my appreciation to You for the gift of this lifetime.

In Jesus' name, I pray.

Amen.

Suggested Oils: Gratitude, Present Time

Awake

Dear God,

Please guide this oil through my physical body and energy field. Awaken me. Clear my mind. Boost my energy and frequency.

In Jesus' name, I pray.

Amen.

Suggested Oils: Awaken, Brain Power, Clarity, Grounding

Blessings

Dear God,

Please guide this oil through my physical body and energy field. Thank you for all of the blessings that surround me. Thank You for blessing me. Let me be a blessing to others.

In Jesus' name, I pray.

Amen.

Suggested Oils: Abundance, Gratitude, Joy, Rose

Cardiovascular System

Dear God,

Please guide this oil through my physical body and energy field, and to each cell of my body. Support my cardiovascular system, and help me to maintain overall wellness.

In Jesus' name, I pray.

Amen.

Suggested Oils: Aroma Life, Frankincense, Golden Rod, Helichrysum, Rosemary

Career

Dear God,

Please guide this oil through my physical body and energy field. Lead me to work that is in alignment with Your Divine Plan. Bless my work, and let my work be a blessing to others.

In Jesus' name, I pray.

Amen.

Suggested Oils: Highest Potential, Joy, Magnify Your Purpose, Oola Field

Clean Eating

Dear God,

Please help the oils to assist me with my commitment to eating clean. Guide me to nourishing foods that replenish my body. Help me to let go of processed foods. Help me to make time to prepare healthy, wholesome foods as you intended us to eat.

In Jesus' name, I pray.

Amen.

Suggested Oils: Awaken, Lavender, Lemon, Lime, Orange, Peppermint, Spearmint

Clarity

Dear God,

Please guide this oil through my physical body and energy field. Clear my mind, my body, and my energy field. Let my thoughts be clear and divinely guided.

In Jesus' name, I pray.

Amen.

Suggested Oils: Brain Power, Clarity, Release, White Angelica

Connection

Dear God,

Please guide this oil through my physical body and energy field. Help me to stay connected to You, and to hold a high frequency. Let me walk in Your Love.

In Jesus' name, I pray.

Amen.

Suggested Oils: Frankincense, Grounding, Sacred Frankincense, Sacred Mountain

Connecting with My Body

Dear God,

Please guide this oil through my body to help me settle into it and feel the energy flowing through me. Help me to love and honor my body. Guide me to foods that nourish and renew my body.

In Jesus' name,

Amen.

Suggested Oils: Grounding, Harmony, Lavender, Rose

Creativity

Dear God,

Please guide this oil through my body and energy field to enhance my creativity. Infuse me with energy and love. Help me to express Your Love in physical form. Help me bring comfort and healing to others with my work.

In Jesus' name,

Amen.

Suggested Oils: Hyssop, Transformation, Wintergreen

Daily Guidance

Dear God,

Please guide this oil through my physical body and energy field. Lead me through my day. Let Your Wisdom attend me in all that I do.

In Jesus' name, I pray.

Amen.

Suggested Oils: Clarity, Grounding, Hong Kuai, Sacred Frankincense

Discernment

Dear God,

Please guide this oil through my physical body and energy field. Help me to see clearly. Infuse me with the Holy Spirit that I may easily discern the truth.

In Jesus' name, I pray.

Amen.

Suggested Oils: Brain Power, Clarity, Exodus II

Divine Timing

Dear God,

Please guide this oil through my physical body and energy field. Help me to align my timing with Divine Timing, and trust that what is for my highest good in alignment with Divine Will is on its way to me.

In Jesus' name, I pray.

Amen.

Suggested Oils: Acceptance, Divine Release, Present Time

Dreams

Dear Heavenly Father,

Please guide this oil through my body and energy field. Help me to bring the dreams you've placed in my heart into reality. Guide my thoughts and actions to create and fulfill my dreams.

In Jesus' name,

Amen.

Suggested Oils: Build Your Dream, Dream Catcher, Highest Potential, Light the Fire

Ears to Hear, Eyes to See

Dear God,

Please guide this oil through my physical body and energy field. Infuse me with the Holy Spirit. Purify my mind, that I may clearly hear You, and easily see the truth.

In Jesus' name, I pray.

Amen.

Suggested Oils: Awaken, Brain Power, Clarity, Grounding, Palo Santo, Present Time, Sacred Frankincense, White Angelica

Energy

Dear God,

Please guide this oil through my body to maintain energy and vitality. Please give me an extra boost of energy and inspiration for the day.

In Jesus' name, I pray.

Amen.

Suggested Oils: Aroma Life, Awaken, En-R-Gee, Motivation, Neroli, Peppermint

Family

Dear God,

Please guide this oil through my physical body and energy field. Protect and shield my family. Keep us connected to each other with love. Help us to maintain a high frequency. Bless my family and all of our loved ones.

In Jesus' name, I pray.

Amen.

Suggested Oils: Gathering, Harmony, Oola Family

Focus

Dear God,

Please guide this oil through my physical body and energy field. Help me daily to stay focused on You. Help me to stay centered and on my path.

In Jesus' name, I pray.

Amen.

Suggested Oils: Clarity, Grounding

Forgiveness

Dear God,

Thank You for the gift of this oil. Please guide this oil through my body and energy field to gently release any past emotions that I may have been harboring. Help me to forgive others and to forgive myself. Help me to release the past and move forward in the light of Your Love.

In Jesus' name,

Amen.

Suggested Oils: Divine Release, Feelings Collection, Forgiveness, Release

Frequency

Dear God,

Please guide this oil through my physical body and energy field. Lift my body and energy field to a high frequency. Help me to hold a high frequency throughout my day and night.

In Jesus' name, I pray.

Amen.

Suggested Oils: Abundance, Exodus II, Forgiveness, Idaho Blue Spruce, Joy, Rose

Gratitude

Dear God,

Please guide this oil through my body and energy field to assist me in seeing all of the beauty around me. Help me to open my heart and express gratitude for the gift of this lifetime.

In Jesus' name,

Amen.

Suggested Oils: Gratitude, Humility

Gratitude for My Body

Dear God,

Please guide this oil through my body and energy field to support harmony in my body. Guide me to self care that nourishes and replenishes my body and energy field. Help me to feel gratitude and love for all parts of my body and being.

In Jesus' name,

Amen.

Suggested Oils: Gratitude, Grounding, Harmony, Rose

Goals

Dear God,

Please guide this oil through my physical body and energy field. Help me to set goals that are in alignment with my purpose. Guide me as I pursue my goals, and help me to take steps towards them each day.

In Jesus' name, I pray.

Amen.

Suggested Oils: Envision, Magnify Your Purpose, Motivation

Grounding

Dear God,

Please guide this oil through my body and energy field to help me anchor my awareness in my body and in this moment. Help me to feel connected to the earth. Help me to be centered and present.

In Jesus' name, I pray.

Amen.

Suggested Oils: Grounding, Lavender, Peace and Calming, Present Time

Guidance

Dear God,

Please guide this oil through my physical body and energy field. Guide me in all aspects of my life. Help me to navigate each day with ease and joy.

In Jesus' name, I pray.

Amen.

Suggested Oils: Believe, Gathering, Highest Potential, Lavender, Present Time

Harmony

Dear God,

Please guide this oil through my physical body and energy field. Bring me into harmony with my purpose. Infuse my life with harmony.

In Jesus' name, I pray.

Amen.

Suggested Oils: Harmony, Highest Potential, Rose

Heart Centered Business

Dear God,

Please guide this oil through my physical body and energy field. Help me to stay connected with my heart and guide me through business transactions.

In Jesus' name, I pray.

Amen.

Suggested Oils: Harmony, Highest Potential, Rose

Highest Potential

Dear God,

Please guide this oil through my body and energy field. Strengthen and invigorate me. Guide me to my highest path and purpose. Illuminate my next steps to achieve my highest potential.

In Jesus' name, I pray.

Amen.

Suggested Oils: Highest Potential, Sacred Frankincense

Hope

Dear God,

Please guide this oil through my body and energy field. Please help me to connect to You and feel Your Love surrounding me. Restore hope in my heart and illuminate my soul.

In Jesus' name, I pray.

Amen.

Suggested Oils: Hope, Joy, Rose, Valor

Immune System

Dear God,

Please guide this oil through my physical body and energy field. Support my immune system. Protect and shield me. Keep me at a high frequency.

In Jesus' name, I pray.

Amen.

Suggested Oils: Cinnamon Bark, Clove, Orange, Oregano, Thieves

Inspiration

Dear God,

Please guide this oil through my physical body and energy field. Fill me with inspiration and purpose. Infuse me with wellness and abundance. Help me to inspire others to live lives of purpose, wellness, and abundance.

In Jesus' name, I pray.

Amen.

Suggested Oils: Envision, Highest Potential, Inspiration, Motivation

Joy

Dear God,

Please uplift my spirit, mind, and body. Guide the oils through all the cells of my body. Lift me to a higher frequency. Help me radiate joy to everyone around me.

In Jesus' name, I pray.

Amen.

Suggested Oils: Joy, Orange, Rose

Life Purpose

Dear God,

Please guide this oil through my body and energy field. Help me to bring purpose to all aspects of my life. Guide me to the reason I incarnated. Help me to align with my soul and higher purpose for this lifetime. Lift me above daily concerns to see the plan for my life. Guide me to take steps each day towards my higher purpose for this lifetime.

In Jesus' name,

Amen.

Suggested Oils: Believe, Build Your Dream, Envision, Hong Kuai, Magnify Your Purpose, Oola Grow

Love

Dear God,

Please guide this oil through my body and energy field to raise my frequency to the frequency of love. Help me to see that love is present in everything you created. May I radiate love to all beings.

In Jesus' name,

Amen.

Suggested Oils: Joy, Rose

Motivation

Dear God,

Please guide this oil through my physical body and energy field. Help me to stay motivated. Boost my daily energy.

In Jesus' name, I pray.

Amen.

Suggested Oils: En-R-Gee, Hong Kuai, Magnify Your Purpose Motivation, Orange, Peppermint

My Gifts

Dear God,

Please guide this oil through my physical body and energy field. Help me to recognize my gifts and talents, and to use them in alignment with Divine Will. May I enhance this world and express Your Love in all that I do.

In Jesus' name, I pray.

Amen.

Suggested Oils: Clarity, Highest Potential, Magnify Your Purpose, Sacred Frankincense

Passion

Dear God,

Please guide this oil through my physical body and energy field. Please reignite my passion and purpose here on Earth. Help me to infuse all aspects of my life with passion.

In Jesus' name, I pray.

Amen.

Suggested Oils: Aroma Life, Inspiration, Jasmine, Joy, Ylang Ylang

On My Father's Planet

Dear Heavenly Father,

Please guide this oil through my physical body and energy field. Help me to see Your Presence in all of creation. Help me to feel Your Love surrounding me and flowing through me. May I reflect Your Love in all that I do.

In Jesus' name, I pray.

Amen.

Suggested Oils: Clarity, Grounding, Frankincense, Northern Lights Black Spruce, Rose, Sacred Frankincense

Open Heart

Dear God,

Please guide this oil through my physical body and energy field. Open my heart to the love and beauty that surrounds me. Help me to be in each moment and experience the love that flows through and around me.

In Jesus' name, I pray.

Amen.

Suggested Oils: Grounding, Harmony, Joy, Present Time, Rose

Peace

Dear God,

Please guide this oil through my body and energy field. Bring peace to my mind, body, and spirit. Help me to remain centered in love. Help me radiate peace to everyone around me.

In Jesus' name, I pray.

Amen.

Suggested Oils: Lavender, Peace and Calming, Peace and Calming II, Tranquil

Positive Life Changes

Dear God,

Please help me to upgrade my habits and thoughts. Assist me in raising my frequency and making consistent steps to uplift my life. Illuminate my path and guide me to become the highest version of myself.

In Jesus' name, I pray.

Amen.

Suggested Oils: Aroma Life, Awaken, Divine Release, Motivation, Release, Transformation

Positive Thought

Dear God,

Please guide this oil through my body and energy field. Raise my frequency. Help me to think positive thoughts and speak positive words. Let my thoughts and words be a blessing.

In Jesus' name, I pray.

Amen.

Suggested Oils: Lavender, Orange, Peppermint, Transformation

Present Moment Awareness

Dear God,

Please guide this oil through my body and energy field to help me focus on this moment. Assist me in occupying my body and being centered in the now. Help me to calm my mind and body. Help me resonate with the peace and aliveness of this moment.

In Jesus' name, I pray.

Amen.

Suggested Oils: Grounding, Peace and Calming, Present Time, Stress Away

Prosperity

Dear God,

Please guide this oil through my body and energy field to raise my frequency and increase my prosperity. Thank You for the abundance you have given me. Help me to embrace the unlimited potential that is within me.

In Jesus' name, I pray.

Amen.

Suggested Oils: Abundance, Ginger, Orange

Protection

Dear God,

Please guide this oil through my physical body and energy field. Adorn me with Your Armor. Place a protective energy field around me. Protect and shield me throughout my day and night.

In Jesus' name, I pray.

Amen.

Suggested Oils: Frankincense, Palo Santo, Sacred Frankincense, Valor, Valor II, White Angelica

Protection

Dear God,

Please guide this oil through my physical body and energy field. Fill my living space with the golden light of the Holy Spirit. Protect and shield my living space throughout the day and night.

In Jesus' name, I pray.

Amen.

Suggested Oils: Frankincense, Palo Santo, Sacred Frankincense, White Angelica

Dear God,

Please guide this oil through my physical body and energy field. Help me to maintain a high frequency. Shield and protect me. Shield and protect my family and friends. Surround us with the golden light of the Holy Spirit.

In Jesus' name, I pray.

Amen.

Suggested Oils: Frankincense, Palo Santo, Sacred Frankincense, Valor, Valor II, White Angelica

Purpose

Dear God,

Please guide this oil through my physical body and energy field. Help me to stay focused on my purpose, and spend time each day on my purpose.

In Jesus' name, I pray.

Amen.

Suggested Oils: Envision, Grounding, Magnify Your Purpose

Release

Dear God,

Please guide this oil through my physical body and energy field. Help me to release the past. Please help my cells and cellular memory to release that which no longer serves me. Help me return to peace and harmony.

In Jesus' name, I pray.

Amen.

Suggested Oils: Divine Release, Forgiveness, Present Time, Release, The Feelings Collection, The Freedom Collection

Releasing Trauma

Dear God,

Please guide this oil through my body to help me release the past. Please help my cells and cellular memory to release anything that no longer serves me. Restore my body and energy field to its original blueprint. Help me return to peace and harmony.

In Jesus' name, I pray.

Amen.

Suggested Oils: Divine Release, Forgiveness, Present Time, Release, The Feelings Collection, The Freedom Collection, Valor, Valor II

Rejuvenation

Dear God,

Please guide this oil through my physical body and energy field, and into each cell of my body. Rejuvenate my mind, my body, and soul.

In Jesus' name, I pray.

Amen.

Suggested Oils: Aroma Life, GLF, Helichrysum, Hinoki, ImmuPower, Lavender

Respiratory System

Dear God,

Please guide this oil through my physical body and energy field. Support my respiratory system. Help me to breathe clearly and easily.

In Jesus' name, I pray.

Amen.

Suggested Oils: Eucalyptus (Globulus or Radiata), Frankincense, Helichrysum, Peppermint, Raven, Ravintsara, R.C., Thieves

Sleep

Dear God,

Please help me to gently relax. Guide the oils into the cells of my body. Help me to release the day, and settle into a deep, rejuvenating sleep. Help me to awaken refreshed and revitalized.

In Jesus' name,

Amen.

Suggested Oils: Lavender, Peace and Calming, Peace and Calming II, RutaVaLa, Valerian

Sleep

Dear God,

Please help these oils to gently relax me. Guide them into the cells of my body. Help me to release the day and settle into a deep, rejuvenating sleep, where my body can heal and restore itself.

In Jesus' name, I pray.

Amen.

Suggested Oils: Lavender, Peace and Calming, Peace and Calming II, RutaVaLa, Valerian

Spiritual Connection

Dear God,

Thank You for guiding this oil through me. Raise my frequency to easily connect with You. Let my daily cares fall away, that I may spend this moment fully present and listening to You.

In Jesus' name, I pray.

Amen.

Suggested Oils: Frankincense, Gratitude, Grounding, Inspiration, Oola Faith, Sacred Frankincense, Sacred Mountain

Surrender

Dear God,

Please guide this oil through my physical body and energy field. Help me to surrender that which no longer serves me and step into my full potential.

In Jesus' name, I pray.

Amen.

Suggested Oils: Divine Release, Release, Surrender

Stress

Dear God,

Please guide this oil through my body and energy field. Calm and soothe me. Help me to be grounded and centered in this moment. Help me to know that all is well. Surround me with Your Love and protection.

In Jesus' name,

Amen.

Suggested Oils: AromaEase, Lavender, Peace and Calming, Peace and Calming II, Stress Away, Tranquil

Synchronicity

Dear God,

Please guide this oil through my physical body and energy field. Help me to recognize synchronicity in my life. Align me with Divine Timing.

In Jesus' name, I pray.

Amen.

Suggested Oils: Grounding, Harmony, Present Time

Synergy

Dear God,

Please guide this oil through my physical body and energy field. Help me to synergize the power of prayer, essential oils, and positivity to maintain a high frequency and enhance my life. Synergize my life with my life's purpose, in alignment with Divine Will.

In Jesus' name, I pray.

Amen.

Suggested Oils: Gathering, Grounding, Harmony, Highest Potential, Sacred Frankincense, Transformation

Thank You

Dear God,

Please guide this oil through my physical body and energy field. Thank You for the blessings you have given me. Thank You for the gift of this lifetime. Thank You for the love that surrounds me.

In Jesus' name, I pray.

Amen.

Suggested Oils: Abundance, Gratitude, Grounding, Present Time

The Gift

Dear God,

Please guide this oil through my physical body and energy field. Thank You for this lifetime. Thank You for Your Love, and blessings. Thank You for Your Presence and guidance. Thank You for walking with me in each moment.

I Love You.

In Jesus' name, I pray.

Amen.

Suggested Oils: Gratitude, Joy, Present Time, Rose, Sacred Frankincense, The Gift

Time

Dear God,

Please guide this oil through my physical body and energy field. Assist me with budgeting my time wisely. Align my priorities with my purpose and help me make the best use of my time.

In Jesus' name, I pray.

Amen.

Suggested Oils: Brain Power, Clarity, Grounding, Present Time

Trust

Dear God,

Please guide this oil through my physical body and energy field. Help me to trust that everything is in alignment with Divine Will. Raise my frequency and help me to walk in love.

In Jesus' name,

Amen.

Suggested Oils: Believe, Idaho Blue Spruce, Rose, Transformation

Truth

Dear God,

Please guide this oil through my physical body and energy field. Clear my mind. Infuse me with the Holy Spirit. Lead me to see the truth in all matters.

In Jesus' name, I pray.

Amen.

Suggested Oils: Brain Power, Clarity, Grounding, Sacred Frankincense, White Angelica

Transformation

Dear God,

Please help this oil to release anything that no longer serves me. Help me transform into the highest version of myself. Please protect and guide me through this transformation.

In Jesus' name,

Amen.

Suggested Oils: Divine Release, Release, Transformation

Unconditional Love

Dear God,

Please guide this oil through my physical body and energy field.
Raise my frequency and help me to feel Your Love for me.
Guide me in loving others unconditionally.

In Jesus' name, I pray.

Amen.

Suggested Oils: Divine Release, Joy, Rose

Walking My Path

Dear God,

Please guide this oil through my physical body and energy field.
Light my path and guide me daily. Help me to walk my path,
and be a shining example of Your Love.

In Jesus' name, I pray.

Amen.

Suggested Oils: Awaken, Build Your Dream, Clarity, Valor

Walking with Our Savior

Dear God,

Please guide this oil through my physical body and energy field. Connect me with my savior, Jesus Christ, and lead me to walk daily with Him.

In Jesus' name, I pray.

Amen.

Suggested Oils: Frankincense, Sacred Frankincense

Wellness

Dear God,

Please guide these oils through my body and energy field. Balance my body and support vibrant wellness.

In Jesus' name,

Amen.

Suggested Oils: Copaiba, Lemon, Lemon Myrtle, Lime, Orange, Neroli

Wellness

Dear God,

Please guide these oils through my body and energy field. Raise my frequency and support my digestive system and my immune system. Please rejuvenate and refresh me.

In Jesus' name,

Amen.

Suggested Oils: Copaiba, Digize, Rose, Thieves

Dear God,

Please guide these oils through my body and energy field. Thank You that all is well with me.

In Jesus' name,

Amen.

Suggested Oils: Abundance, Gratitude, Joy, Northern Lights Black Spruce, Rose

Single Oils

I included a few prayers that correspond with popular single essential oils and a couple of my favorite single essential oils. Additional prayers with corresponding single oils and blends can be found in my book – Moments of Reflection.

Frankincense

Dear God,

Please guide this blessed oil - Frankincense - through my body and energy field. Support vibrant wellness throughout my mind, body, and soul.

In Jesus' name, I pray.

Amen.

* Frankincense can be diffused or applied while meditating.

Lavender

Dear God,

Please guide this oil - Lavender - through my body and energy field. Guide the oil to where it is most needed. Bless me, and let me be a blessing to others.

In Jesus' name, I pray.

Amen.

Lavender

Dear God,

Please guide this gentle oil of Lavender through my body. Help me relax and let go of stress.

In Jesus' name,

Amen.

Lavender

Dear God,

Please guide this Lavender oil through all aspects of me. Restore and rejuvenate me, and prepare me for a deep, restful night of sleep.

In Jesus' name,

Amen.

Lemon

Dear God,

Please guide Lemon essential oil through my body and energy field. Help me to gently cleanse and detox my body. Please assist me with shifting to healthy choices.

In Jesus' name,

Amen.

Northern Lights Black Spruce

Dear God,

Please guide this oil – Northern Lights Black Spruce- through my body and energy field. Infuse me with the electrical charge of the Northern Lights. Surround me with the fragrance of the woods.

In Jesus' name, I pray.

Amen.

Orange

Dear God,

Please guide Orange oil through my body and energy field. Support my immune system and uplift me.

In Jesus' Name,

Amen.

Peppermint

Dear God,

Please guide this oil - Peppermint – through my body and energy field. Energize and uplift me. Please help the oil to clear my mind and refresh me.

In Jesus' Name,

Amen.

Peppermint

Dear God,

Please guide this oil - Peppermint - through my body and energy field. Please calm and soothe my digestive system.

In Jesus' name, I pray.

Amen.

Sacred Frankincense

Dear God,

Please guide this blessed oil – Sacred Frankincense - through my body and energy field. Deepen my connection with You. May I walk each day with You.

In Jesus' name, I pray.

Amen.

* Sacred Frankincense can be diffused or applied while meditating.

Conclusion

I hope that the time spent in prayer and reflection while applying the oils has brought you to a deeper connection with yourself and with God. Life is a gift. Being present and aware of this moment helps you to experience the fullness of the moment and of life. Being present in your body makes it easier to be in the present moment versus thinking about the past or always focusing on the future. The best way to create the future you want is to be fully present now.

Connecting with God daily also helps you to be in the present moment and fully appreciate your time here on Earth. Staying connected to God also helps to maintain a high frequency and a clear energy field. A clear mind, body, and energy field helps with wellness, purpose, and abundance. Living a lifestyle that supports wellness, purpose, and abundance helps you to fulfill your purpose here.

I trust that the prayers I have included express my love for the oils and Our Creator. His Love for each and every one of us can be found in the gift of essential oils. May you walk in love.

Blessings,

Jennie M. Fuller

YL Member #1757073

Website: www.ylbewell.com

Email: jenniefuller@ylbewell.com

Suggested Reading

Essential Oils Desk Reference

 or Pocket Reference book by Life Science Publishing

Healing Oils of the Bible by David Stewart, Ph.D.

The Chemistry of Essential Oils Made Simple: God's Love Manifest in Molecules by David Steward, Ph.D.

The One Gift by D. Gary Young

Additional copies of this book are available on Amazon or Createspace at: https://www.createspace.com/5966682

Moments of Reflection (prayers for single oils and blends) is available on Amazon or on Lulu at: www.lulu.com/spotlight/jenniefuller

32080651R20033

Made in the USA
San Bernardino, CA
28 March 2016